To:
_____

From:
_____

Promises

A Bouquet of Promises

Published by Garborg's Heart 'n Home, Inc.
P. O. Box 20132, Bloomington, MN 55420

Photography copyright © by Virginia Dixon
Designed by Mick Thurber

Except for Scriptures, references to "men" and
masculine pronouns have been replaced with
"women" or "people" and feminine pronouns.

SPCN 5-5044-0210-7

Promises

Always new. Always
exciting. Always full of
promise. The mornings
of our lives, each a
personal daily miracle!

GLORIA GAITHER

January 1

Promises

There are better things
ahead than any we
leave behind.

C. S. LEWIS

December 31

Promises

May God's richest
blessings be upon you
both today and throughout
the year—and may those
blessings flow through
you to touch the lives
of everyone you meet.

GARY SMALLEY

January 2

Promises

The Dayspring from on
high has visited us; to give
light...to guide our feet
into the way of peace.

LUKE 1:78,79 ·NKJV·

December 30

Promises

What lies behind us,
and what lies before us
are tiny matters, compared
to what lies within us.

RALPH WALDO EMERSON

January 3

Promises

If we celebrate the years
behind us they become
stepping stones of
strength and joy for
the years ahead.

December 23

Promises

This is the day the Lord
has made. We will rejoice
and be glad in it.

PSALM 118:24 TLB

January 4

Promises

Recall it as often as you
wish, a happy memory
never wears out.

LIBBIE FUDIM

December 28

Promises

Every day in a life fills the
whole life with expectation
and memory.

C. S. LEWIS

January 5

Promises

God peace is joy resting.
His joy is peace dancing.

F. F. BRUCE

December 27

Promises

Each dawn holds a
new hope for a new plan,
making the start of each
day the start of a new life.

GINA BLAIR

January 6

Promises

Glory to God in the
highest, and on earth
peace to men on whom
his favor rests.

LUKE 2:14 NIV

December 26

Promises

God is the beginning—
not just the starting
point, but the source
of all things.

MARILYN M. MORGAN

January 7

Promises

Christmas is the
celebration of the
keeping of a promise.
A saving promise.

MICHAEL CARD

December 25

Promises

I wish you sunshine on
your path and storms to
season your journey. I wish
you peace in the world in
which you live and in the
smallest corner of the heart
where truth is kept.... More
I cannot wish you except
perhaps love to make all
the rest worthwhile.

ROBERT A. WARD

January 8

Promises

The magical dust
of Christmas glittered
on the cheeks of humanity
ever so briefly, reminding
us of what is worth
having and what we were
intended to be.

MAX LUCADO

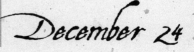

December 24

Promises

For the soul of
every living thing is in
the hand of God, and the
breath of all mankind.

JOB 12:10 TLB

January 9

Promises

God grant you the light
in Christmas, which is
faith; the warmth of
Christmas, which is
love...the all of Christmas,
which is Christ.

WILDA ENGLISH

December 23

Promises

Life, love, and laughter—
what priceless gifts!

January 10

Promises

Jesus—
Light of the world.
Joy of our hearts.

December 22

Promises

God knows the rhythm of
my spirit and knows my
heart thoughts. He is as
close as breathing.

January 11

Promises

For to us a child is born, to us a son is given, and the government will be on his shoulders. And he will be called Wonderful Counselor, Mighty God, Everlasting Father, Prince of Peace.

ISAIAH 9:6 NIV

December 21

Promises

Happiness is found
along the way, not at
the end of the road.

January 12

Promises

It is good to be children
sometimes, and never
better than at Christmas,
when its mighty Founder
was a child himself.

CHARLES DICKENS

December 20

Promises

The Lord will keep you from all harm—he will watch over your life; the Lord will keep your going out and your coming in from this time on and forevermore.

PSALM 121:7,8 NRSV

January 13

Promises

Christ is the still point of
the turning world.

T. S. ELIOT

December 19

Promises

Every day holds the
possibility of a miracle.

January 14

Promises

The heart of the giver
makes the gift dear
and precious.

MARTIN LUTHER

December 18

Promises

Be on the lookout
for mercies. The more
we look for them, the
more of them we will see.
Blessings brighten when
we count them.

MALTBIE D. BABCOCK

January 15

Promises

The virgin will be with
child and will give birth to
a son, and they will call
him Immanuel—which
means, "God with us."

MATTHEW 1:23 NIV

December 17

Promises

To have a friend is to have
one of the sweetest gifts
that life can bring.

AMY ROBERTSON BROWN

January 16

Promises

For somehow, not only
at Christmas, but all the
year through, the joy you
give to others is the joy
that comes back to you.

JOHN GREENLEAF WHITTIER

December 16

Promises

There is no joy in life like
the joy of sharing.

BILLY GRAHAM

January 17

Promises

Happiness is being at
peace, being with loved
ones, being comfortable.
But most of all, it's having
those loved ones.

JOHNNY CASH

December 15

Promises

But I keep right on
praying to you, Lord.
For now is the time—
you are bending down to
hear! You are ready with
a plentiful supply of love
and kindness.

PSALM 69:13 TLB

January 18

Promises

It is more blessed
to give than to receive—
so much more blessed!

December 14

Promises

I asked God for all things
that I might enjoy life. He
gave me life that I might
enjoy all things.

January 19

Promises

God gave us memories
so that we might have
roses in December.

JAMES M. BARRIE

December 13

Promises

The things that matter
the most in this world,
they can never be
held in our hand.

GLORIA GAITHER

January 20

Promises

Thanks be to God for
his indescribable gift!

2 CORINTHIANS 9:15 NIV

December 12

Promises

A true friend is a gift
of God, and only He
who made hearts can
unite them.

January 21

Promises

God is every moment
totally aware of each one
of us. Totally aware in
intense concentration
and love.

EUGENIA PRICE

December 11

Promises

The Lord is faithful to all
his promises and loving
toward all he has made....
You open your hand and
satisfy the desires of
every living thing.

PSALM 145:13,16 NIV

January 22

Promises

A thing of beauty is
a joy forever.

JOHN KEATS

December 10

Promises

Today well lived makes
every yesterday a dream
of happiness and every
tomorrow a vision
of hope.

January 23

Promises

Do what you can,
with what you have,
where you are.

THEODORE ROOSEVELT

December 9

Promises

May you grow to be as
beautiful as God meant
you to be when He first
thought of you.

January 24

Promises

Anyone who loves God
is known by him.

1 Corinthians 8:3 NRSV

December 8

Promises

Faith expects from
God what is beyond
all expectation.

<small>ANDREW MURRAY</small>

January 25

Promises

Act as if each day
were given to you for
Christmas, just as eager,
just as proud.

December 7

Promises

Time has a wonderful
way of showing us what
really matters.

January 26

Promises

Somewhere on the
great world the sun is
always shining, and it will
sometimes shine on you.

MYRTLE REED

December 6

Promises

You created my
inmost being; you
knit me together in my
mother's womb. I praise
you because I am fearfully
and wonderfully made;
your works are wonderful,
I know that full well.

PSALM 139:13,14 NIV

January 27

Promises

Spread your love
everywhere you go.

MOTHER TERESA

December 5

Promises

The time to be happy
is now; the place to
be happy is here.

ROBERT G. INGERSOLL

January 28

Promises

We may depend upon
God's promises, for
He will be as good
as His word.

MATTHEW HENRY

December 4

Promises

Faith in small things has
repercussions that ripple all
the way out. In a huge,
dark room a little match
can light up the place.

JONI EARECKSON TADA

January 29

Promises

I have loved you
with an everlasting love;
I have drawn you with
loving-kindness.

JEREMIAH 31:3 NIV

December 3

Promises

God is, and all is well.

JOHN GREENLEAF WHITTIER

January 30

Promises

I will honor Christmas
in my heart and try to
keep it all year.

CHARLES DICKENS

December 2

Promises

My Father gives me new
life—not just for today,
but for tomorrow and
every day after that.

January 31

Promises

When you have
accomplished your daily
task, go to sleep in peace.
God is awake.

Victor Hugo

December 1

Promises

May the Lord be loyal to
you...and reward you with
many demonstrations
of his love!

2 SAMUEL 2:6 TLB

February 1

Promises

Our thanksgiving today
should include those things
which we take for granted.

BETTY FUHRMAN

November 30

Promises

Love has its source in
God, for love is the very
essence of His being.

KAY ARTHUR

February 2

Promises

Oh, give thanks to
the Lord, for he is good;
His love and his kindness
go on forever.

1 CHRONICLES 16:34 NIV

November 23

Promises

God loves and cares for us, even to the least event and smallest need of life.

HENRY EDWARD MANNING

February 3

Promises

I would maintain that
thanks are the highest
form of thought, and that
gratitude is happiness
doubled by wonder.

G. K. CHESTERTON

November 28

Promises

The secret to enjoying life
is to be thankful for what
each day brings.

February 4

Promises

There is always something
for which to be thankful.

CHARLES DICKENS

November 27

Promises

Love is extravagant in
the price it is willing to
pay, the time it is willing
to give, the hardships
it is willing to endure,
and the strength it is
willing to spend.

JONI EARECKSON TADA

February 5

Promises

Thanksgiving is a time of quiet reflection upon the past and an annual reminder that God has, again, been ever so faithful. The solid and simple things of life are brought into clear focus.

CHARLES R. SWINDOLL

November 26

Promises

The Lord gives strength to
his people; the Lord blesses
his people with peace.

PSALM 29:11 NIV

February 6

Promises

Gratitude.
More aware of what you
have than what you don't.
Recognizing the treasure
in the simple—a child's
hug, fertile soil, a golden
sunset. Relishing in the
comfort of the common.

MAX LUCADO

November 25

Promises

Originality is not doing
something no one else
has ever done, but doing
what has been done
countless times with
new life, new breath.

MARIE CHAPIAN

February 7

Promises

To be grateful is to
recognize the love of
God in everything He has
given us—and He has
given us everything.
Every breath we draw
is a gift of His love.

THOMAS MERTON

November 24

Promises

May God give you eyes to
see beauty only the heart
can understand.

February 8

Promises

In everything give thanks.

1 Thessalonians 5:18 nasb

November 23

Promises

What do we live for,
if not to make the
world less difficult
for each other?

GEORGE ELIÓT

February

Promises

Seeing our Father in
everything makes life one
long thanksgiving and
gives a rest of heart.

HANNAH WHITALL SMITH

November 22

Promises

Life gives you the
chance to love, to work,
to play, and to look up
at the stars.

HENRY VAN DYKE

February 10

Promises

The hand that gives,
gathers.

ENGLISH PROVERB

November 21

Promises

Many blessings are
given to those who
trust the Lord.

PSALM 40:4 TLB

February 11

Promises

There is something in
every season, in every
day, to celebrate with
thanksgiving.

GLORIA GAITHER

November 20

Promises

Life is so full of meaning
and purpose, so full of
beauty—beneath its
covering—that you
will find that earth but
cloaks your heaven.

FRA GIOVANNI

February 12

Promises

O give thanks to the
Lord, for he is good;
for his steadfast love
endures forever.

PSALM 107:1 NRSV

November 19

Promises

Great works do not always
lie in our way, but every
moment we may do little
ones excellently, that is,
with great love.

FRANCIS DE SALES

February 13

Promises

You have a unique
message to deliver, a unique
song to sing, a unique act
of love to bestow. This
message, this song, and
this act of love have been
entrusted exclusively to
the one and only you.

JOHN POWELL, S. J.

November 18

Promises

Love knows no limit to
its endurance, no end
to its trust, no fading
of its hope; it can
outlast anything.

1 CORINTHIANS 13:8 Phillips

February 14

Promises

God's friendship is the
unexpected joy we find
when we reach His
outstretched hand.

JANET L. WEAVER

November 17

Promises

As high as the heavens
are above the earth, so
great is his love.

PSALM 103:10 NIV

February 15

Promises

Love is not getting, but
giving.... It is goodness and
honor and peace and pure
living—yes, love is that
and it is the best thing in
the world and the thing
that lives the longest.

HENRY VAN DYKE

November 16

Promises

Kind words can be
short and easy to speak,
but their echoes are
truly endless.

MOTHER TERESA

February 16

Promises

Thank you, Lord! How
good you are! Your love for
us continues on forever.
Who can ever list the
glorious miracles of God?

PSALM 106:1,2 TLB

November 15

Promises

Whatever we have is
worth twice as much
when we share it.

February 17

Promises

We have been in God's
thought from all eternity,
and in His creative love,
His attention never
leaves us.

MICHAEL QUOIST

November 14

Promises

Flowers leave their
fragrance on the hand
that bestows them.

CHINESE PROVERB

February 18

Promises

God is constantly taking
knowledge of me in love
and watching over me
for my good.

J. I. PACKER

November 13

Promises

The Lord will fulfill his
purpose for me; your love,
O Lord, endures forever.

<small>PSALM 138:8 NIV</small>

February 19

Promises

Remember this—that
very little is needed to
make a happy life.

MARCUS AURELIUS

November 12

Promises

How beautiful a day
can be when kindness
touches it.

February 20

Promises

May you be ever present
in the garden of His love.

November 11

Promises

Hope is not a granted wish or a favor performed.... It is a zany, unpredictable dependence on a God who loves to surprise us out of our socks.

MAX LUCADO

February 21

Promises

The heavens declare the
glory of God; the skies
proclaim the work
of his hands.

PSALM 19:1 NIV

November 10

Promises

If peace be in the heart
the wildest winter storm
is full of solemn beauty.

C. F. RICHARDSON

February 22

Promises

Were there no God, we
would be in this glorious
world with grateful hearts
and no one to thank.

Christina Rossetti

November 9

Promises

God's bright sunshine
overhead, God's flowers
beside your feet...and by
such pleasant pathways led,
may all your life be sweet.

HELEN WRAITHMAN

February 23

Promises

No matter how late
the hour, no matter how
desperate the moment, we
cannot despair; the joy and
riches God has promised
us stretch like a shining
road into the future!

CATHERINE MARSHALL

November 8

Promises

So I commend the enjoyment of life, because nothing is better for a man under the sun than to eat and drink and be glad. Then joy will accompany him in his work all the days of the life God has given him under the sun.

ECCLESIASTES 8:15 NIV

February 24

Promises

Loving and being loved
is the greatest of
human joys.

<small>EDWARD E. FORD</small>

November 7

Promises

God's love imparts
its own loveliness until
one day we shall be
altogether lovely.

DR. HENRY JEWETT

February 25

Promises

May the Lord, the God of
your fathers, increase you a
thousand times and bless
you as he has promised!

DEUTERONOMY 1:11 NIV

November 6

Promises

Memories, important
yesterdays, were once
todays. Treasure and
notice today.

GLORIA GAITHER

February 26

Promises

Love comes out of heaven
unasked and unsought.

PEARL S. BUCK

November 5

Promises

Write on your heart
that every day is the
best day of the year.

RALPH WALDO EMERSON

February 27

Promises

Those who bring
sunshine to the lives
of others cannot keep
it from themselves.

JAMES M. BARRIE

November 4

Promises

You pay God a
compliment by asking
great things of Him.

TERESA OF AVILA

February 28

Promises

Happiness is itself
a kind of gratitude.

JOSEPH W. KRUTCH

November 3

Promises

He will feed his flock like
a shepherd; he will carry
the lambs in his arms.

ISAIAH 40:11 TLB

February 29

Promises

The great acts of love
are done by those who
are habitually performing
small acts of kindness.

November 2

Promises

Friends...they cherish
each other's hopes.
They are kind to each
other's dreams.

HENRY DAVID THOREAU

March 1

Promises

May God our Father...
mightily bless each one of
you, and give you peace.

2 Corinthians 1:2 tlb

November 1

Promises

Love doesn't make the
world go round. Love is
what makes the ride
worthwhile.

FRANKLIN P. JONES

March 2

Promises

If there is anything
better than to be loved,
it is loving.

October 31

Promises

We are ordinary people
with an extraordinary God.

March 3

Promises

It is only with the heart
that one can see rightly.
What is essential is
invisible to the eye.

ANTOINE DE SAINT-EXÚPERY

October 30

Promises

Ask, and you will be
given what you ask for.
Seek, and you will find.
Knock, and the door will
be opened. For everyone
who asks, receives. Anyone
who seeks, finds. If only
you will knock, the
door will open.

MATTHEW 7:7,8 TLB

March 4

Promises

Far away, there in the sunshine, are my highest aspirations.... I can look up and see their beauty, believe in them, and try to follow where they lead.

LOUISA MAY ALCOTT

October 29

Promises

You can never do a
kindness too soon, because
you never know how soon
it may be too late.

March 5

Promises

May the God of hope fill
you with all joy and peace
in believing, that you may
abound in hope.

ROMANS 15:13 · NKJV

October 28

Promises

I am beginning to learn
that it is the sweet, simple
things of life which are
the real ones after all.

LAURA INGALLS WILDER

March 6

Promises

Peace is when time doesn't
matter as it passes by.

MARIA SCHNELL

October 27

Promises

Look for the heaven
here on earth. It is
all around you.

March 7

Promises

If you invest in beauty,
it will remain with you all
the days of your life.

FRANK LLOYD WRIGHT

October 26

Promises

May you wake each day
with God's blessings and
sleep each night in His
keeping, and may you
always walk in His
tender care.

March 8

Promises

God has a wonderful
plan for each person.
He knew even before He
created this world what
beauty He would bring
forth from our lives.

LOUIS B. WYLY

October 25

Promises

Your heavenly Father
knows your needs. He will
always give you all you
need from day to day.

Luke 12:30,31 TLB

March 9

Promises

God goes to those who
come to Him.

RUSSIAN PROVERB

October 24

Promises

Thank God for
regular days.

<small>GLORIA GAITHER</small>

March 10

Promises

Be glad for all God
is planning for you.
Be patient...and
prayerful always.

ROMANS 12:12 TLB

October 23

Promises

Every morning is a fresh
opportunity to find God's
extraordinary joy in the
most ordinary places.

JANET L. WEAVER

March 11

Promises

From there to here, and
here to there, funny things
are everywhere.

DR. SEUSS

October 22

Promises

To me, every hour
of the day and night
is an unspeakably
perfect miracle.

WALT WHITMAN

March 12

Promises

The beauty of the
sunbeam lies partly in
the fact that God does
not keep it; He gives it
away to us all.

DAVID SWING

October 21

Promises

The Lord...richly blesses
all who call on him.

ROMANS 10:12 NIV

March 13

Promises

The future belongs to
those who believe in the
beauty of their dreams.

ELEANOR ROOSEVELT

October 20

Promises

There is always a time
for gratitude and
new beginnings.

J. ROBERT MOSKIN

March 14

Promises

From the fullness of his
grace we have all received
one blessing after another.

JOHN 1:16 NIV

October 19

Promises

By love alone is God
enjoyed; by love alone
delighted in; by love alone
approached and admired.
His nature requires love.

THOMAS TRAHERNE

March 15

Promises

Know that you yourself
are a miracle.

NORMAN VINCENT PEALE

October 18

Promises

Every person's life is
a fairy tale written by
God's fingers.

HANS CHRISTIAN ANDERSEN

March 16

Promises

God's fingers can touch
nothing but to mold it
into loveliness.

GEORGE MACDONALD

October 17

Promises

May life's greatest gifts
always be yours—
happiness, memories,
and dreams.

March 17

Promises

Something deep in all of
us yearns for God's beauty,
and we can find it no
matter where we are.

SUE MONK KIDD

October 16

Promises

Rejoice in the Lord
always. I will say it
again: Rejoice!

PHILIPPIANS 4:4 NIV

March 18

Promises

Stand outside this
evening. Look at the stars.
Know that you are special
and loved by the One
who created them.

October 15

Promises

Where love is,
God is also.

LEO TOLSTOY

March 19

Promises

If you give, you will get!
Your gift will return to
you in full and overflowing
measure, pressed down,
shaken together to make
room for more, and
running over.

LUKE 6:38 TLB

October 14

Promises

Our lives are filled
with simple joys and
blessings without end,
And one of the greatest
joys in life
is to have a friend.

March 20

Promises

It is good to let a little sunshine out as well as in.

October 13

Promises

Contentment is not the
fulfillment of what you
want, but the realization
of how much you
already have.

March 21

Promises

Happiness always looks
small while you hold it in
your hands, but let it go,
and you learn at once how
big and precious it is.

MAKSIM GORKY

October 12

Promises

So be truly glad!
There is wonderful joy
ahead, even though the
going is rough for a
while down here.

1 PETER 1:6 TLB

March 22

Promises

If we knew the power
of kindness, we should
transform this world
into a paradise.

CHARLES WAGNER

October 11

Promises

Add to your joy
by counting your
blessings.

March 23

Promises

With God everything
is possible.

MARK 10:27 TLB

October 10

Promises

The soul can split the sky
in two, and let the face of
God shine through.

EDNA ST. VINCENT MILLAY

March 24

Promises

Love is, above all,
the gift of oneself.

JEAN ANOUILH

October

Promises

God loves us;
not because we are lovable
but because He is love,
not because He needs to
receive, but because He
delights to give.

C. S. LEWIS

March 25

Promises

Nothing is so strong
as gentleness, nothing so
gentle as real strength.

FRANCIS DE SALES

October 8

Promises

When you were born,
God said, "Yes!"

March 26

Promises

Nothing can separate
you from God's love,
absolutely nothing....
God is enough for time,
God is enough for eternity.
God is enough!

HANNAH WHITALL SMITH

October 7

Promises

Every good and perfect
gift is from above, coming
down from the Father of
the heavenly lights, who
does not change like
shifting shadows.

JAMES 1:17 NIV

March 27

Promises

Some people make the
world special just by
being in it.

October 6

Promises

You are tenderly loved by
the One who created you.

JANET L. WEAVER

March 28

Promises

The Lord your God...will
take great delight in you,
he will quiet you with his
love, he will rejoice over
you with singing.

ZEPHANIAH 3:17 NIV

October 5

Promises

Kindness always blesses
the heart of the giver.

March 29

Promises

Love is a fruit in season
at all times and within the
reach of every hand.

MOTHER TERESA

October 4

Promises

I want to learn to live
each moment and be
grateful for what it brings,
asking no more.

GLORIA GAITHER

March 30

Promises

Sharing with another is
a simple way to say...we
need each other.

JANET L. WEAVER

October 3

Promises

Peace is seeing a sunset
and knowing who
to thank.

March 31

Promises

Life is short and we
never have enough time
for the hearts of those
who travel the way with us.
O, be swift to love!
Make haste to be kind.

HENRI FRÉDÉRIC AMIEL

October 2

Promises

Whatever you do,
do it with kindness
and love.

1 CORINTHIANS 16:14 TLB

April 1

Promises

What a wonderful God
we have—he is...the
source of every mercy,
and the one who so
wonderfully comforts
and strengthens us.

2 CORINTHIANS 1:3,4 TLB

October 1

Promises

As Jesus stepped into the garden, you were in His prayers. As Jesus looked into heaven, you were in His vision.... His final prayer was about you. His final pain was for you. His final passion was you.

MAX LUCADO

April 2

Promises

My friend shall forever
be my friend and reflect
a ray of God to me.

HENRY DAVID THOREAU

September 30

Promises

All the flowers of
tomorrow are in the
seeds of today.

April 3

Promises

Appreciate the goodness
of God. Count your
blessings. Learn not
to take pleasures
for granted.

J. I. PACKER

September 29

Promises

Blessed are the ones God
sends to show His love
for us—our friends.

April 4

Promises

Peace within makes
beauty without.

ENGLISH PROVERB

September 28

Promises

Jesus cannot forget us;
we have been graven on
the palm of His hands.

LOIS PICILLO

April 5

Promises

Blessed are those
who hold their earthly
possessions in open palms.

MAX LUCADO

September 27

Promises

I will send down showers
in season; there will be
showers of blessing.

EZEKIEL 34:26 NIV

April 6

Promises

The steadfast love of
the Lord never ceases, his
mercies never come to an
end; they are new every
morning; great is your
faithfulness.

LAMENTATIONS 3:22,23 NRSV

September 26

Promises

God puts each fresh
morning, each new
chance of life, into our
hands as a gift to see
what we will do with it.

April 7

Promises

Our brightest blazes
of gladness are
commonly kindled by
unexpected sparks.

SAMUEL JOHNSON

September 25

Promises

God's forgiveness and love
exist for you as if you were
the only person on earth.

CECIL OSBORNE

April 8

Promises

Kind words are jewels that
live in the heart and soul
and remain as blessed
memories years after they
have been spoken.

MARVEA JOHNSON

September 24

Promises

God's promises are
written on every leaf
of springtime.

April

Promises

Faith makes all things
possible. Hope makes all
things bright. Love makes
all things easy.

September 23

Promises

We know that in all things
God works for the good of
those who love him.

ROMANS 8:28 NIV

April 10

Promises

To love and to be loved
is a blessing that keeps
on giving.

September 22

Promises

May happiness touch
your life today as warmly
as you have touched the
lives of others.

April 11

Promises

In quietness and trust
is your strength....
The Lord longs to be
gracious to you; he rises
to show you compassion.
For the Lord is a God of
justice. Blessed are all
who wait for him!

Isaiah 30:15,18 NIV

September 21

Promises

Let us believe that God
is in all our simple
deeds and learn to
find Him there.

A. W. TOZER

April 12

Promises

Memories are perhaps
the best gifts of all.

GLORIA GAITHER

September 20

Promises

Joy is the echo of God's
life within us.

JOSEPH MARMION

April 13

Promises

Remember that what you
now have was once among
the things only hoped for.

EPICURUS

September 19

Promises

The good for which we are
born into this world is that
we may learn to love.

GEORGE MACDONALD

April 14

Promises

Every little blessing is far
too precious to ever forget
to say "thank you!"

September 18

Promises

I will not forget you.
See, I have inscribed you
on the palm of my hands.

Isaiah 49:15,16 nrsv

April 15

Promises

The eternal God is your
refuge, and underneath are
the everlasting arms.

DUETERONOMY 33:27 NIV

September 17

Promises

Seeds of kindness will
yield a bountiful harvest
of blessings.

April 16

Promises

We make a living by what we get, but we make a life by what we give.

WINSTON S. CHURCHILL

September 16

Promises

The heavenly Father
welcomes us with open
arms and imparts to us
blessing upon blessing.

April 17

Promises

If it's nothing more than
a smile—give that away
and keep on giving it.

BETH BROWN

September 15

Promises

Blessed are those
who can give without
remembering and take
without forgetting.

ELIZABETH BIBESCO

April 18

Promises

Each day is a little life.
Live it to the fullest.

September 14

Promises

For, lo, the winter is past,
the rain is over and gone;
the flowers appear on the
earth; the time of the
singing of birds is come.

SONG OF SOLOMON 2:11,12 KJV

April 19

Promises

Blessed are they who
can laugh at themselves,
for they shall never
cease to be amused.

September 13

Promises

Jesus' love does not depend
upon what we do for Him.
Not at all. In the eyes of
the King, you have value
simply because you are.

MAX LUCADO

April 20

Promises

To enjoy your work and
to accept your lot in life—
that is indeed a gift from
God. The person who does
that will not need to look
back with sorrow on
his past, for God
gives him joy.

ECCLESIASTES 5:20 TLB

September 12

Promises

God bless you
and utterly satisfy your
heart with himself.

AMY CARMICHAEL

April 21

Promises

Friends give full color
to our lives; they help us
sharpen our focus, giving
a clearer picture of all the
beautiful, simple things
that really matter.

September 11

Promises

You are in the Beloved,
therefore infinitely dear
to the Father, unspeakably
precious to Him. You
are never, not for one
second, alone.

NORMAN F. DOWTY

April 22

Promises

God has put something
noble and good into every
heart His hand created.

MARK TWAIN

September 10

Promises

Never lose an opportunity
of seeing anything that is
beautiful; for beauty is
God's handwriting.

RALPH WALDO EMERSON

April 23

Promises

To understand and to be
understood makes our
happiness on earth.

GERMAN PROVERB

September 9

Promises

How precious it is,
Lord, to realize that you
are thinking about me
constantly! I can't even
count how many times
a day your thoughts
turn towards me.

PSALM 139:17 TLB

April 24

Promises

He who refreshes others
will himself be refreshed.

PROVERBS 11:25 NIV

September 8

Promises

May a rainbow be certain
to follow each rain;
May the hand of a friend
always be near you;
May God fill your heart
with gladness to cheer you.

IRISH BLESSING

April 25

Promises

He loves each one of us,
as if there were only
one of us.

AUGUSTINE

September 7

Promises

When seeds of kindness
are sown prayerfully in the
garden plot of our lives we
may be sure that there will
be a bountiful harvest of
blessings both for us
and for others.

W. PHILLIP KELLER

April 26

Promises

The happiness of life
is made of little things—
a smile, a hug, a moment
of shared laughter.

September 6

Promises

Having someone who
understands is a great
blessing for ourselves.
Being someone who
understands is a great
blessing to others.

JANETTE OKE

April 27

Promises

We walk without fear, full
of hope and courage and
strength to do His will,
waiting for the endless
good which He is always
giving as fast as He can
get us able to take it in.

GEORGE MACDONALD

September 5

Promises

Lift up your eyes.
The heavenly Father
waits to bless you—in
inconceivable ways to make
your life what you never
dreamed it could be.

ANNE ORTLUND

April 28

Promises

May only good things
come your way every
moment of today.

September 4

Promises

Abiding love surrounds
those who trust in the
Lord. So rejoice in him,
all those who are his, and
shout for joy, all those
who try to obey him.

PSALM 32:10,11 TLB

April 29

Promises

The Lord's blessing is
our greatest wealth.

PROVERBS 10:22 TLB

September 3

Promises

Most smiles are started
by another smile.

April 30

Promises

Be simple; take our
Lord's hand and walk
through things.

FATHER ANDREW SDC

September 2

Promises

God, who is love...
simply cannot help but
shed blessing upon blessing
upon us. We do not need
to beg, for He simply
cannot help it!

HANNAH WHITALL SMITH

May 1

Promises

All I have seen teaches me
to trust the Creator for all
I have not seen.

RALPH WALDO EMERSON

September 1

Promises

The best things are
nearest: breath in your
nostrils, light in your eyes,
flowers at your feet, duties
at your hand, the path of
God just before you.

ROBERT LOUIS STEVENSON

May 2

Promises

Since we are his
children, we will share
his treasures—for all God
gives to his Son Jesus
is now ours too.

ROMANS 8:17 TLB

August 31

Promises

Every moment is full
of wonder, and God is
always present.

May 3

Promises

Time, indeed, is a sacred
gift, and each day is
a little life.

JOHN LUBBOCK

August 30

Promises

From the rising of the
sun to the place where it
sets, the name of the Lord
is to be praised.... Who is
like the Lord our God,
the One who sits
enthroned on high.

PSALM 113:3,5 NIV

May 4

Promises

His joy is in those who
reverence him, those
who expect him to be
loving and kind.

PSALM 147:11·NIV

August 29

Promises

Take spring when it
comes and rejoice. Take
happiness when it comes,
and rejoice. Take love when
it comes, and rejoice.

CARL EWALD

May 5

Promises

One of life's greatest
treasures is the love that
binds hearts together
in friendship.

August 28

Promises

Every gift of kindness
bears the signature of love.

JANET L. WEAVER

May 6

Promises

Our Creator would never
have made such lovely days
and have given us the deep
hearts to enjoy them,
above and beyond all
thought, unless we were
meant to be immortal.

NATHANIEL HAWTHORNE

August 27

Promises

May I never miss a sunset
or a rainbow because I am
looking down.

May 7

Promises

The Lord gives you
the experience of enjoying
His presence. He touches
you, and His touch is so
delightful that, more than
ever, you are drawn
inwardly to Him.

MADAME JEAN GUYON

August 26

Promises

He surrounds me with
lovingkindness and tender
mercies. He fills my life
with good things!

PSALM 103:4,5 TLB

May 8

Promises

May the Lord continually
bless you with heaven's
blessings as well as with
human joys.

PSALM 128:5 TLB

August 25

Promises

Today's bright moments
are tomorrow's fond
memories.

May 9

Promises

God is the God of
promise. He keeps His
word, even when it seems
impossible; even when
the circumstances point
to the opposite.

COLIN URQUHART

August 24

Promises

Time is a very precious
gift of God; so precious
that it's only given to us
moment by moment.

AMELIA BARR

May 10

Promises

There is no surprise
more magical than the
surprise of being loved.
It is the finger of God
on our shoulder.

<small>MARGARET KENNEDY</small>

August 23

Promises

What the heart has once owned and had, it shall never lose.

HENRY WARD BEECHER

May 11

Promises

Happiness comes of the
capacity to feel deeply,
to enjoy simply, to think
freely, to risk life,
to be needed.

SAMUEL JAMESON

August 22

Promises

Life is God's gift to you.
The way you live your life
is your gift to God. Make
it a fantastic one.

LEO BUSCAGLIA

May 12

Promises

Nothing we can do
will make the Father
love us less. He loves
us unconditionally with
an everlasting love. All
He asks of us is that we
respond to Him with
the free will that He
has given to us.

NANCIE CARMICHAEL·

August 21

Promises

Because the Lord is
my Shepherd, I have
everything I need! He lets
me rest in meadow grass
and leads me beside the
quiet streams. He gives
me new strength.

PSALM 23:1-3 TLB

May 13

Promises

Joy rises in my heart
until I burst out in songs
of praise to him.

PSALM 28:7 TLB

August 20

Promises

True worth is in being,
not seeming—
In doing, each day
that goes by,
Some little good—
not in dreaming
Of great things to do
by and by.

ALICE CARY

May 14

Promises

Live to shed joys
on others.

HENRY WARD BEECHER

August 19

Promises

All that is worth
cherishing begins
in the heart.

SUZANNE CHAPIN

May 15

Promises

God will never let you
be shaken or moved from
your place near His heart.

JONI EARECKSON TADA

August 18

Promises

Within your heart
Keep one still, secret spot
Where dreams may go
And, sheltered so,
May thrive and grow.

LOUISE DRISCOLL

May 16

Promises

Happiness held is the
seed; happiness shared
is the flower.

August 17

Promises

Taste and see that
the Lord is good.

PSALM 34:8 NIV

May 17

Promises

Lord, you have examined
my heart and know
everything about me....
You both precede and
follow me, and place your
hand of blessing on my
head. This is too glorious,
too wonderful to believe!

PSALM 139:1,5,6 TLB

August 16

Promises

The greatest gift is a
portion of yourself.

RALPH WALDO EMERSON

May 18

Promises

You are a child of your
heavenly Father. Confide
in Him. Your faith in His
love and power can never
be bold enough.

BASILEA SCHLINK

August 15

Promises

That I am here
is a wonderful mystery
to which I will respond
with joy.

May 19

Promises

It seems so simple appreciating life for what it is—pleasure and pain, joy and sorrow. For the moment, for today at least, I have learned to be content.

GLORIA GAITHER

August 14

Promises

To love someone
means to see her as
God intended her.

FEODOR DOSTOEVSKY

May 20

Promises

How beautiful it is
to be alive!

HENRY SEPTIMUS SUTTON

August 13

Promises

Nobody has measured,
even poets, how much
a heart can hold.

ZELDA FITZGERALD

May 21

Promises

God understands our
prayers even when we
can't find the words
to say them.

August 12

Promises

O [Lord]...your
lovingkindness is
wonderful; your mercy
is so plentiful, so tender
and so kind.

PSALM 69:16 TLB

May 22

Promises

May you be blessed by
the Lord, the Maker of
heaven and earth.

PSALM 115:15 NIV

August 11

Promises

We can make up our
minds whether our lives
in this world shall be
beautiful and fragrant
like the lilies of the field.

FATHER ANDREW SDC

May 23

Promises

Remember that happiness
is a way of travel—
not a destination.

ROY M. GOODMAN

August 10

Promises

The greatest use of life is
to spend it for something
that will outlast it.

WILLIAM JAMES

May 24

Promises

Some blessings—like
rainbows after rain or a
friend's listening ear—
are extraordinary gifts
waiting to be discovered
in an ordinary day.

August 9

Promises

The best and most
beautiful things in the
world cannot be seen or
even touched. They must
be felt with the heart.

HELEN KELLER

May 25

Promises

His tenderness in
the springing grass,
His beauty in the flowers,
His living love in the
sun above—
All here, and near,
and ours.

<small>CHARLOTTE PERKINS GILMAN</small>

August 8

Promises

Be beautiful inside,
in your hearts, with the
lasting charm of a gentle
and quiet spirit which is
so precious to God.

1 PETER 3:4 TLB

May 26

Promises

He is like a father to us,
tender and sympathetic....
The lovingkindness of the
Lord is from everlasting
to everlasting to those
who reverence him.

PSALM 103:13,17 TLB

August 7

Promises

Blossoms are scattered
by the wind and the wind
cares nothing, but the
blossoms of the heart
no wind can touch.

YOSHIDA KENKO

May 27

Promises

It is a fine seasoning
for joy to think of
those we love.

Molière

August 6

Promises

Live your life while you have it. Life is a splendid gift—there is nothing small about it.

FLORENCE NIGHTINGALE

May 28

Promises

The Lord's goodness
surrounds us at every
moment. I walk through
it almost with difficulty,
as through thick grass
and flowers.

R. W. BARBER

August 5

Promises

The secret of life is that
all we have and are is a gift
of grace to be shared.

Lloyd John Ogilvie

May 29

Promises

The things that count
the most cannot
be counted.

August 4

Promises

The wind rushing
through the grass, the
thrush in the treetops,
and children tumbling in
senseless mirth stir in us
a bright faith in life.

DONALD CULROSS PEATTIE

May 30

Promises

I have a heart with room
for every joy.

P. J. BAILEY

August 3

Promises

Where your pleasure is,
there is your treasure;
where your treasure,
there your heart; where
your heart, there
your happiness.

AUGUSTINE

May 31

Promises

May God be gracious to
us and bless us and make
his face shine upon us.

PSALM 67:1 NIV

August 2

Promises

Great is your love,
reaching to the heavens;
your faithfulness reaches
to the skies. Be exalted,
O God, above the heavens;
let your glory be over
all the earth.

PSALM 57:10,11 NIV

June 1

Promises

All perfect gifts are
from above and all our
blessings show
The amplitude of
God's dear love which any
heart may know.

LAURA LEE RANDALL

August 1

Promises

The goodness of God is
infinitely more wonderful
than we will ever be able
to comprehend.

A. W. TOZER

June 2

Promises

Delight yourself in the
surprises of today!

July 31

Promises

It isn't the big pleasures
that count the most; it's
making a great deal out
of the little ones.

JEAN WEBSTER

June 3

Promises

Every single act of love
bears the imprint of God.

July 30

Promises

You have made known
to me the paths of life;
you will fill me with joy
in your presence.

ACTS 2:28 NIV

June 4

Promises

My God is changeless
in his love for me.

PSALM 59:10 TLB

July 29

Promises

Faith believes that God
will plant the seeds of hope
for tomorrow in the garden
of our hearts today.

JANET L. WEAVER

June 5

Promises

Joy is a light that fills
you with hope and
faith and love.

ADELA ROGERS ST. JOHNS

July 28

Promises

It is the simple things
of life that make living
worthwhile, the sweet
fundamental things such
as love and duty, work
and rest, and living
close to nature.

LAURA INGALLS WILDER

June 6

Promises

The sun does not shine
for a few trees and
flowers, but for the
wide world's joy.

HENRY WARD BEECHER

July 27

Promises

A friend is a gift whose
worth cannot be measured
except by the heart.

June 7

Promises

A kind heart is a
fountain of gladness,
making everything in
its vicinity freshen
into smiles.

WASHINGTON IRVING

July 26

Promises

One of the most
wonderful things about
knowing God is that
there's always so much
more to know, so much
more to discover.

JONI EARECKSON TADA

June 8

Promises

God loves us, and the will
of love is always blessing
for its loved ones.

HANNAH WHITALL SMITH

July 25

Promises

Let the hearts of those who seek the Lord rejoice. Look to the Lord and his strength; seek his face always. Remember the wonders he has done.

PSALM 105:3-5 NIV

June 9

Promises

When we obey him,
every path he guides us
on is fragrant with his
lovingkindness and
his truth.

PSALM 25:10 TLB

July 24

Promises

Your greatest pleasure
is that which rebounds
from hearts that you
have made glad.

HENRY WARD BEECHER

June 10

Promises

He made you so
you could share in His
creation, could love and
laugh and know Him.

TED GRIFFEN

July 23

Promises

We have not made
ourselves; we are the
gift of the living God
to one another.

REINE DUELL BETHANY

June 11

Promises

Miracles happen to those
who believe in them.

BERNARD BERENSON

July 22

Promises

We are so very rich
if we know just a few
people in a way in which
we know no others.

CATHERINE BRAMWELL-BOOTH

June 12

Promises

Love is the reason
behind everything
God does.

July 21

Promises

I will praise you, O Lord,
with all my heart; I will tell
of all your wonders. I will
be glad and rejoice in you.

PSALM 9:1,2 NIV

June 13

Promises

You have welcomed me
as your guest; blessings
overflow! Your goodness
and unfailing kindness
shall be with me all
of my life.

PSALM 23:5,6 TLB

July 20

Promises

The greatest gift we
can give one another is
rapt attention to one
another's existence.

SUE ATCHLEY EBAUGH

June 14

Promises

God is as great in
minuteness as He
is in magnitude.

July 19

Promises

Only a life lived for others
is the life worthwhile.

ALBERT EINSTEIN

June 15

Promises

You are God's created
beauty and the focus of
His affection and delight.

JANET L. WEAVER

July 18

Promises

God is not too great
to be concerned about
our smallest wishes.

BASILEA SCHLINK

June 16

Promises

A friend is the hope
of the heart.

RALPH WALDO EMERSON

July 17

Promises

A friend may well be
reckoned the masterpiece
of nature.

RALPH WALDO EMERSON

June 17

Promises

Some people may see
the first bright rays of
sunshine stretching across
the sky. I see my Father's
smile, greeting me at the
start of a new day!

July 16

Promises

Let them thank the Lord
for his steadfast love, for
his wonderful works to
humankind. For he
satisfies the thirsty,
and the hungry he fills
with good things.

PSALM 107:8,9 NRSV

June 18

Promises

The Lord will guide
you always; he will satisfy
your needs.... You will be
like a well-watered garden,
like a spring whose
waters never fail.

ISAIAH 58:11 NIV

July 15

Promises

He is right here.
With an unyielding
desire that is willing to
trust, you may boldly call
out to God and know
that He will answer.

June 19

Promises

The time you spend
caring today will be a love
gift that will blossom into
the fresh joy of God's
Spirit in the future.

EMILIE BARNES

July 14

Promises

No love, no friendship
can cross the path of our
destiny without leaving
some mark on it forever.

FRANÇOIS MAURIAC

June 20

Promises

Be glad you had
the moment.

STEVE SHAGAN

July 13

Promises

Take time to notice the
usually unnoticed, simple
things in life. Delight in
the never-ending hope
that's available every day!

June 21

Promises

Among God's best gifts
to us are the people
who love us.

July 12

Promises

See Jesus in everything
and in everything you
will find a blessing.

June 22

Promises

You have made known
to me the path of life;
you will fill me with joy
in your presence, with
eternal pleasures at
your right hand.

PSALM 16:11 NIV

July 11

Promises

Kind words are like
honey—enjoyable
and healthful.

PROVERBS 16:24 TLB

June 23

Promises

Reach high, for stars
lie hidden in your soul.
Dream deep, for every
dream precedes the goal.

PAMELA VAULL STARR

July 10

Promises

Our happiness is greatest
when we contribute most
to the happiness of others.

HARRIET SHEPARD

June 24

Promises

God's hand is always
there; once you grasp
it, you'll never want
to let it go.

July

Promises

God never abandons
anyone on whom He
has set His love; nor does
Christ the Good Shepherd
ever lose track of
His sheep.

J. I. PACKER

June 25

Promises

We think God's love
rises and falls with our
performance. It doesn't.
He loves you for whose
you are: you are His child.

MAX LUCADO

July 8

Promises

Everyone was meant to
share God's all-abiding
love and care; He saw
that we would need to
know a way to let these
feelings show....
So God made hugs.

JILL WOLF

June 26

Promises

The Lord your God is
the faithful God who for
a thousand generations
keeps his promises and
constantly loves those
who love him and who
obey his commands.

DEUTERONOMY 7:9 TLB

July 7

Promises

Lovely flowers are the
smiles of God's goodness.

WILBERFORCE

June 27

Promises

Friendship is precious,
not only in the shade,
but in the sunshine
of life as well.

THOMAS JEFFERSON

July 6

Promises

The Lord bless you and
keep you; the Lord make
his face shine upon you
and be gracious to you; the
Lord turn his face toward
you and give you peace.

NUMBERS 6:24-26 NIV.

June 28

Promises

Your only treasures are
those which you carry
in your heart.

DEMOPHILUS

July 5

Promises

God's promise of love
and life everlasting reaches
far beyond the scope of
my imagination.

June 29

Promises

Pay attention to the small
things—the kite flies
because of its tail.

<small>Hawaiian Proverb</small>

July 4

Promises

The gift of happiness
belongs to those who
unwrap it.

June 30

Promises

Light tomorrow
with today!

ELIZABETH BARRETT BROWNING

July 3

Promises

Every day under the sun
is a gift. Receive it with
eagerness. Treat it kindly.
Share it with joy. Each
night return it to the Giver
who will make it bright
and shiny again before
the next sunrise.

July 1

Promises

If...you seek the Lord your
God, you will find him if
you look for him with all
your heart and with
all your soul.

DEUTERONOMY 4:29 NIV

July 2